**Bible Readers Series**

## A Study of Psalms

# LIVING IN GOD'S PRESENCE

## Pat Floyd

Abingdon Press / Nashville

**LIVING IN GOD'S PRESENCE**
**A STUDY OF PSALMS**

＊

ISBN 0-687-09256-6

ISBN 978-0-687-09256-7

07 08 09 10—10 9 8 7
Manufactured in the United States of America.

# CONTENTS

### Chapter One

# CELEBRATING THE GIFT OF LIFE

## PURPOSE
To help us celebrate the wonder of creation and the wisdom of God the Creator

## BIBLE PASSAGE
**Psalm 104:24-34**

24 O LORD, how manifold are your works!
   In wisdom you have made them all;
   the earth is full of your creatures.
25 Yonder is the sea, great and wide,
   creeping things innumerable are there,
   living things both small and great.
26 There go the ships,
   and Leviathan that you formed to sport in it.

27 These all look to you
   to give them their food in due season;
28 when you give to them, they gather it up;
   when you open your hand,
      they are filled with good things.
29 When you hide your face, they are dismayed;
   when you take away their breath, they die
   and return to their dust.

30 **When you send forth your spirit, they are created;
and you renew the face of the ground.**

31 **May the glory of the LORD endure forever;
may the LORD rejoice in his works—**
32 **who looks on the earth and it trembles,
who touches the mountains and they smoke.**
33 **I will sing to the LORD as long as I live;
I will sing praise to my God
while I have being.**
34 **May my meditation be pleasing to him,
for I rejoice in the LORD.**

---

**CORE VERSE**

*O LORD, how manifold are your works!
In wisdom you have made them all;
the earth is full of your creatures.*
*(Psalm 104:24)*

---

## OUR NEED

Where do you feel truly a part of God's creation: serene, joyful, and delighted to be alive? Most people would like to spend more time in such places. But the demands of work and family, the restrictions of illness and physically challenging conditions, or the habit of focusing on indoor activities prevents many of us from doing so. We miss the first daffodils of spring, wrens nesting, the majesty of mountains and ocean, tomatoes from a garden, the glory of autumn leaves, the silhouette of bare branches against a winter sunset.

Circumstances of life today leave many people feeling divorced from creation, no longer at home in the universe. Often, we do not realize what we are missing until we take a vacation, go on a retreat, or just spend time in the back yard or in a park. Then we sense that for our own health and wholeness, we need to be related to the natural world.

When we think about God's creation, we may also feel anxiety, grief, frustration, and guilt. We may wonder how much longer we will be able to enjoy beauty we once took for granted and how much longer the earth will have the resources needed to sustain life as we know it. We may grieve for lost trees and open spaces, for lost farms, and for birds and animals that once were familiar neighbors. We may feel frustration at the difficulty of finding just and effective ways to care for the earth and to provide for human beings. And we may feel guilt that we have not done everything in our power to be good stewards of creation.

*What feelings does contemplation of God's creation evoke in you?*

## FAITHFUL LIVING

Psalms are poetry. They are hymns and sometimes prayers. To understand and appreciate a psalm, begin by reading it aloud; get a feel for the meaning of the psalmist's words. Psalm 104 is a joy to read aloud. Give yourself the pleasure, at some time, of reading the entire psalm. It describes God's creation of the earth and God's wisdom and care in providing for all creatures, including human beings.

In the portion of the psalm for our study, verses 24-26 praise God for the vast number of things God has created and for the wisdom with which God has made them all. Verses 27-30 speak of the dependence of all creation on God. Verses 31-32 praise God's glory and God's power. Verses 33-34 are the psalmist's response to God in praise and in prayer for a life that will be pleasing to God.

In our study of Psalm 104, we need to note that the people of Israel had no concept of nature as we view it or of the Greek idea of cosmos. The Hebrew language of the Scriptures does not convey ideas of the earth and the universe as self-contained, ordered structures, subject to study and objective analysis by human beings. For the people of Israel, Creation was an act of God. Their experience of the world around them was a personal awareness of being present in the midst of evidence of God's actions in the past and of God's continuing activity in the present.

In considering the Psalms as a whole, the biblical scholar Gerhard von Rad spoke of the Psalms as "Israel in the presence of [God]." The Book of Psalms is a collection of songs, prayers, and Wisdom teachings that were most often sung or spoken when the people of Israel gathered for worship and celebrations. Like all Scripture, the Psalms address the whole people of God and express the people's praise, petitions, and response to God. However, some psalms clearly began as hymns that individuals addressed to God. Psalm 104 is such a psalm.

*What role do the Psalms have in your life and in the worship of your congregation?*

## Proclaim God's Greatness

> O LORD, how manifold are your works!
>     In wisdom you have made them all;
>     the earth is full of your creatures.
>                                        (Psalm 104:24)

The psalmist lived in the midst of God's creation, observed it with care, and was filled with awe at the number and variety of the creatures God has made.

Verse 25 speaks of the sea filled with innumerable things, both small and great. The truth of that statement was brought home to me on a visit to the Aquarium of the Americas in New Orleans. From the 350 known species of the shark family, we saw some sharks that were less than a foot long, others that were huge, and a model of the whale shark that grows to 40 feet in length. Size, color, body shape, and diet of the sharks vary greatly to fit the habitat of each species.

The fish that most impressed me with the wonder of creation, however, were those that looked like the work of a fine artist. Usually, they were small fish. Handsome white or silver fish were covered with intricate geometric patterns, meticulously drawn in black. Other fish looked like swimming jewels—scarlet, lapis blue, gold, orange, and lemon yellow. Sometimes an area of color or a stripe was outlined with a fine black line.

*Intention* and *delight* are the words my aquarium visit brings to mind. Attention to details that permit each species to function superbly, to adapt to its habitat, and to survive speaks to my faith in a God who creates with infinite care and purpose for the good of all. The beauty of the created world speaks to me of a God who delights in creation. Small fish could surely be created with the ability to find food, to mate, and to hide from predators without their being exquisitely beautiful as well. Indeed, "the LORD rejoice[s] in his works" (verse 31b).

The Creator who takes delight in each creature has also created them to take delight in their own living. The psalmist speaks of God's forming Leviathan to sport in the sea (verse 26). Leviathan is usually thought to be a sea monster, but I wonder if the psalmist could have been thinking of the play of whales.

In verse 32 the psalmist recognizes the power of God in the terrible, the awe inspiring, and the destructive. God is the one

> who looks on the earth and it trembles,
> who touches the mountains and they smoke.

For the psalmist all creation comes from God and is to be accepted as evidence of God's wisdom, power, and greatness.

*What aspects of creation speak to you most eloquently of the Creator? What aspects, if any, test your faith in God's goodness?*

## Acknowledge Our Dependence

Psalm 104 takes for granted the total dependence of all creatures on God's provision:

> When you open your hand,
>   they are filled with good things.
> When you hide your face, they are dismayed;
>   when you take away their breath, they die
>   and return to their dust.
>                     (Psalm 104:28b-29)

Because we are able to affect conditions of life and health and the productivity of the earth, we sometimes lose sight of our dependence on what God has provided. Fertile topsoil, clean water and air, and solar energy are essential for life. Remove or seriously diminish any one of them and life ends. Furthermore, we are born as creatures; we live our lives in plenty and scarcity, sickness and health; and we die.

The psalmists accepted the cycles of life and death as a part of God's creation while still lamenting the transitoriness of life. They found assurance in God's continuing presence and in the continuity of life:

> Long ago you laid the foundation of the earth,
>   and the heavens are the work of your hands.
> They will perish, but you endure;
>   they will all wear out like a garment.
> You change them like clothing, and they pass away;
>   but you are the same, and your years have no end.
> The children of your servants shall live secure;
>   their offspring shall be established in your
>     presence.
>                     (Psalm 102:25-28)

To accept death as a part of God's good plan for creation is not easy when faced with the death of anyone or anything we hold dear. Yet, in the service for Ash Wednesday, I usually feel a sense of peace when the words are repeated to me, "Remember that you are dust, and to dust you shall return. Praise be to God." I think that peace comes from God's grace expressed in Jesus' words, "I am the resurrection and the life. Those who believe in me, even though they die, will live, and everyone who lives and believes in me will never die" (John 11:25-26).

Psalm 104 reveals God's affirmation of life in all its diversity and complexity, its abundance and deprivation, its rejoicing, and its loss. Verse 30 affirms that God also continues to renew and to recreate life:

> When you send forth your spirit, they are created;
>    and you renew the face of the ground.

This theme appears—and is carried even further—in the writings of the prophets and in Paul's epistles, where the redemption of God's people is related to the restoration of all creation:

> The wolf and the lamb shall feed together,
>    the lion shall eat straw like the ox. . . .
> They shall not hurt or destroy
>    on all my holy mountain,
>       says the LORD.
>
> (Isaiah 65:25)

"The creation itself will be set free from its bondage to decay and will obtain the freedom of the glory of the children of God" (Romans 8:21).

*In what ways is our complete dependence on God's provision for us troubling? In what ways is it reassuring?*

## Rejoice in God's Creation

> I will sing to the LORD as long as I live;
> I will sing praise to my God while I have being.
>
> (Psalm 104:33)

Praise is the psalmist's first response to God's wisdom and goodness in creation. What shall our responses be? Four responses seem especially appropriate: to cherish what God has made, to take delight in it, to praise God, and to live a life that is pleasing to God and in harmony with God's creative work.

Few people would set a wet coffee cup on a friend's just-completed painting, throw garbage in a neighbor's front yard, or pour poison in a child's goldfish bowl. Yet many people are careless and even wanton in their disregard for God's creation.

In *The Diversity of Life,* biologist Edward O. Wilson voices the belief that humanity has initiated a great extinction of life on earth in which a large fraction of our fellow species will be wiped out in a single generation. His contention is that every scrap of biological diversity is priceless, to be studied and cherished; and his plea is that not one form of life be given up without a struggle. How can Christians pray, "May the LORD rejoice in his works" (Psalm 104:31) if we do not acknowledge God as Creator by respecting and preserving what God has made?

In contrast to those who carelessly mar and destroy are two friends of mine. They count each morning glory blossom at their door and touch each one with tenderness because the life of each blossom is short and must be celebrated and appreciated each day. Once they lifted a dying butterfly from the gutter and held it gently until it was forever still because such a lovely thing should not die alone. Where there is life, someone should care and take notice.

We can delight in God's creation by seeing it; by hearing

it; by smelling, touching, and tasting it. Whether we are beholding a house plant, a giant sequoia, or a display of vegetables in the grocery store, we can celebrate God's creative hand at work. Life is too short to turn aside from a glorious sunset or to ignore a bird's song. When we are aware of life, we are more fully alive.

We can praise God for creation with songs, prayers, and Scripture. I recommend that for the rest of this study you give yourself the joy of praising God with psalms about creation. Besides Psalm 104, Psalm 8 speaks of our place in creation, Psalm 19 of the heavens telling God's glory, Psalm 33 of how God created, Psalm 65 of crops and harvest, Psalm 147 of winter's snow, and Psalm 96 and Psalm 148 of how all things praise God. Praise God and express your delight in the creation with your own poetry, prose, or music and with arts of all kinds.

The psalmist also wrote,

> May my meditation be pleasing to him,
> for I rejoice in the LORD.
>> (Psalm 104:34)

He saw his whole life as a song of praise to God. Should we not see our lives the same way?

---

**CLOSING PRAYER**

O God, help us live our lives in loving care for one another and for all creation, celebrating with our choices, our words, and our actions the life you have given us. In the name of the One who bestows abundant life, Jesus Christ, we pray. Amen.

---

**Chapter Two**

# REMEMBER PROMISES AND COMMITMENTS

### PURPOSE
To help us recall and give praise for God's acts of blessing and deliverance

### BIBLE PASSAGE
**Psalm 105:1-11, 43-45**

1 O give thanks to the LORD, call on his name,
    make known his deeds among the peoples.
2 Sing to him, sing praises to him;
    tell of all his wonderful works.
3 Glory in his holy name;
    let the hearts of those who seek
        the LORD rejoice.
4 Seek the LORD and his strength;
    seek his presence continually.
5 Remember the wonderful works he has done,
    his miracles, and the judgments
        he has uttered,
6 O offspring of his servant Abraham,
    children of Jacob, his chosen ones.

7 He is the LORD our God;
    his judgments are in all the earth.

8 He is mindful of his covenant forever;
    of the word that he commanded,
      for a thousand generations,
9 the covenant that he made with Abraham,
    his sworn promise to Isaac,
10 which he confirmed to Jacob as a statute,
    to Israel as an everlasting covenant,
11 saying, "To you I will give the land of Canaan
    as your portion for an inheritance."...

43 So he brought his people out with joy,
    his chosen ones with singing.
44 He gave them the lands of the nations,
    and they took possession of
      the wealth of the peoples,
45 that they might keep his statutes
    and observe his laws.
    Praise the LORD!

---

**CORE VERSE**

*O give thanks to the LORD, call on his name,*
*make known his deeds among the peoples.*
*(Psalm 105:1)*

---

## OUR NEED

Members of a small group from my church read Psalm 105. Each of us was to tell about one of God's wonderful works we had witnessed or experienced. Since the whole group was feeling discouraged about what was happening in our world, we lamented together a bit before we were ready for rejoicing and praise. (Lamenting as well as praise is a theme of the Psalms.) When we were ready to speak of God's wonderful deeds, our remembering and sharing was an exceedingly rewarding experience for all of us.

Some told stories of healing; some, of reconciliation; and others, of vocational guidance. We remembered what has happened in the life of our church and were uplifted by the histories we shared. Our unanimous reaction was, "We, and our whole church, need to do this on a regular basis." We wanted to remember and to celebrate our common history as a congregation of God's people and our individual parts in that story.

As people of God, all of us need to remember and to celebrate God's wonderful deeds and God's continuing promises to us.

## FAITHFUL LIVING

Psalm 105 is a hymn of praise for God's mighty acts in fulfilling God's covenant with the people of Israel. Verses 1-6 call the assembled people to proclaim what God has done and to praise God. Verses 7-11 introduce the main theme of the psalm: God's covenant with the people and the fulfilling of the covenant. Verses 12-42, which are not a part of our lesson, recount the history of God's leading and delivering the people. Verses 43-45 tell how God's promise was fulfilled and what God expects of the people in response.

Each year the people of Israel went on pilgrimage to Jerusalem to celebrate three great festivals: the Festival of Booths or Tabernacles, at harvest time in the fall; the Passover Festival celebrating deliverance from Egypt, in the spring; and the Feast of Weeks or first fruits, at the time of the wheat harvest. Psalm 105 was probably used at these festivals.

In 1 Chronicles 16, we have a record of Psalm 105:1-15 being used in worship. David prepared a place for the ark of God and brought it up to Jerusalem in a procession of Levites and people. The placing of the ark was celebrated with sacrifices, feasting, music, and songs of thanksgiving. First Chronicles 16:7 reads, "On that day David first appointed the singing of praises to the LORD by Asaph and his kindred." Psalm 105:1-15 is then given as the first part of what was sung.

## Remember God's Covenant

Israel identified itself as a people with whom God had made an everlasting covenant, as God's servant. In Israel a servant was one who belonged to another and who was supported and protected as a part of that person's household. Israel had been chosen by God to belong to God's household. God's promise to give Israel the land of Canaan may have been viewed as being like the promise of land as an inheritance.

However, no human relationships can describe adequately the importance for Israel of God's initiative in choosing them, making a covenant with them, freeing them from slavery in Egypt, and leading them to the Promised Land. Psalm 100:3 suggests that God created Israel as a people:

> Know that the LORD is God.
>> It is he that made us, and we are his;
>> we are his people, and the sheep
>> of his pasture.

Psalm 105 identifies God's covenant with Abraham as the beginning of God's relationship with Israel. God appeared to Abraham in Haran and said, "Go from your country and your kindred and your father's house to the land that I will show you" (Genesis 12:1). God then made a covenant with Abraham and later with Isaac. God also appeared to Isaac's son Jacob in a dream and confirmed the covenant: "I am the LORD, the God of Abraham your father and the God of Isaac; the land on which you lie I will give to you and to your offspring; and your offspring shall be like the dust of the earth" (Genesis 28:13-14).

The covenant had four parts: the promise of land, the promise of descendants who would continue to participate in the covenant, the promise that Israel would be a blessing to other peoples, and the promise of God's continuing presence and protection. Over the years, the people affirmed their identity as offspring of Abraham, Isaac, and Jacob. For them, God's covenant was not ancient history; it was a present and living reality.

Yet when the Hebrews were slaves in Egypt, the hope of the covenant and the presence of the God of the covenant must have seemed remote. God's announcement to Moses at the burning bush, "I am the God of your father, the God of Abraham, the God of Isaac, and the God of Jacob" (Exodus 3:6), was an identification that suggested a reaffirmation of God's promises.

And so it was. God said,

I have remembered my covenant. Say therefore to the Israelites, "I am the LORD, and I will free you from the burden of the Egyptians and deliver you from slavery to them. I will redeem you with an outstretched arm and with mighty acts of judgment. I will take you as my people, and I will be your God. You shall know that I am the LORD your God, who has freed you from the burdens of the Egyptians. I will bring you into the land that I swore to give to Abraham, Isaac, and Jacob; I will give it to you for a possession. I am the LORD."

(Exodus 6:5-8)

Psalm 105 recounts the steps by which God delivered the people from Egypt and from their wilderness wanderings. Then it concludes by celebrating the fulfillment of God's promise:

So he brought his people out with joy,
    his chosen ones with singing.
He gave them the lands of the nations,
    and they took possession of
    the wealth of the peoples.

(Psalm 105:43-44)

**Praise God's Wonderful Deeds**

Psalm 78 and Psalm 106 recount many of the same events as Psalm 105, but they dwell on Israel's sin and faithlessness in response to God's gracious acts. Psalm 105, on the other hand, focuses entirely on God's wonderful deeds and on praising God for the covenant fulfilled. In spite of everything that is wrong with us and with the world, as God's people we need to center at times on remembering the power and grace of God's presence among us. We need to rejoice in God's continuing promises and purposes for us.

Psalm 105 begins with strong imperatives: "Give thanks to the LORD," "call on his name," "sing praises to him," "glory in his holy name." One scholar suggests that the phrase translated "call on his name" in the NRSV might be more accurately translated "call out his name." The psalm calls us to join together in exuberant praise. Singing hymns both in public worship and alone is a wonderful way to praise God.

We are not only to sing God's praises but to "make known his deeds among the peoples" (verse 1) and to remember and to tell "the wonderful works he has done" (verse 5). The people of Israel were to remember and to tell God's deeds, not just for their own benefit, but so the nations around them would know what God had done. In God's covenant all the nations of the earth would be blessed through Israel.

Psalm 105:3b-4 further commands,

> Let the hearts of those who seek
> the LORD rejoice.
> Seek the LORD and his strength;
> seek his presence continually.

The people of Israel needed God's strength and God's presence in order to live out God's purpose for them. God had given them the Promised Land that they might "keep his statutes / and observe his laws" (verse 45).

The law was God's gift to Israel: "What other great nation

has statutes and ordinances as just as this entire law that I am setting before you today?" (Deuteronomy 4:8). In obeying God's law, Israel would be God's people, a holy nation and a light to the nations.

So now, O Israel, what does the LORD your God require of you? Only to fear the LORD your God, to walk in all his ways, to love him, to serve the LORD your God with all your heart and with all your soul, and to keep the commandments of the LORD your God and his decrees that I am commanding you today, for your own well-being.

(Deuteronomy 10:12-13)

Obedience to the law was the seal of God's covenant with Israel and Israel's ultimate act of praise.

*How will you praise God for God's grace active in your life?*

### Celebrate God's Promises to Us

As Christians, we are God's people, Abraham's descendants, and inheritors of the covenant. We, and those who come after us, have the covenant assurance that God will be with us. We have Jesus' promise, "I am with you always, to the end of the age" (Matthew 28:20b). We have Paul's testimony that "neither death, nor life, nor angels, nor rulers, nor things present, nor things to come, nor powers, nor height, nor depth, nor anything else in all creation, will be able to separate us from the love of God in Christ Jesus our Lord" (Romans 8:38-39).

All the families of the earth are blessed through the heritage of the people of Israel. In Christ that covenant blessing becomes explicit. Christ sends us into all the world to make disciples of all nations and to tell the good news that God loved the world so much that he sent his only Son into the world that through him the world might be saved.

We do not claim the covenant promise of a homeland on earth, but Christ invites us to enter the kingdom of God. In this Kingdom the first are last, the servant is most highly honored, the least of God's children is welcomed, and sinners and tax collectors are not turned away. We have great cause for celebration!

*How does your congregation celebrate God's promises?*

---

**CLOSING PRAYER**
Sing praise to God
   who reigns above,
the God of all creation,
the God of power,
   the God of love,
the God of our salvation.
With healing balm
   my soul is filled and
every faithless murmur stilled:
To God all praise and glory.[1]

---

[1] From "Sing Praise to God Who Reigns Above," in *The United Methodist Hymnal* (Copyright © 1989 The United Methodist Publishing House); 126.

### Chapter Three

# WHEN TROUBLE COMES

### PURPOSE
To encourage us to rely upon God in times of trouble

### BIBLE PASSAGE
Psalm 34:2-10, 18-22

2 My soul makes its boast in the LORD; *NIV*
   let the humble hear and be glad." *let the afflicted hear and rejoice*

3 O magnify the LORD with me,
   and let us exalt his name together.

4 I sought the LORD, and he answered me,
   and delivered me from all my fears.

5 Look to him, and be radiant;
   so your faces shall never be ashamed.

6 This poor soul cried, and was
         heard by the LORD,
   and was saved from every trouble.

7 The angel of the LORD encamps
      around those who fear him,
         and delivers them.

8 O taste and see that the LORD is good;
   happy are those who take refuge in him.

*NIV "blessed"*

9 O fear the LORD, you his holy ones,
   for those who fear him have no want.
10 The young lions suffer want and hunger,
   but those who seek the LORD
      lack no good thing. . . .

18 The LORD is near to the brokenhearted,
   and saves the crushed in spirit.
19 Many are the afflictions of the righteous,
   but the LORD rescues them
      from them all.
20 He keeps all their bones;
   not one of them will be broken.
21 Evil brings death to the wicked,
   and those who hate the righteous will be
      condemned.
22 The LORD redeems the life of his servants;
   none of those who take refuge in him
      will be condemned.

---

**CORE VERSE**

*The LORD is near to the brokenhearted,
and saves the crushed in spirit.*

*(Psalm 34:18)*

---

## OUR NEED

The title of this lesson is "*When* Trouble Comes," not "*If* Trouble Comes." Each person reading these words has known trouble; and, undoubtedly, each of us will face trouble again.

Among the persons sitting near me at church on the day I began writing this lesson, three have a child with serious substance abuse problems; one has a daughter who has recently served a jail sentence; and another's son has dropped out of school. One woman is trying to survive the aftermath of rape and a divorce she does not want. A man is struggling with depression.

Any gathering of people could probably name a similar collection of adversities. We could add physical illness, bereavement, and problems associated with aging—three of our most frequent sources of concern.

The writer of Ecclesiastes took a pessimistic view of life's troubles. He wrote, "I saw all the oppressions that are practiced under the sun. Look, the tears of the oppressed—with no one to comfort them! . . . And I thought the dead, who have already died, more fortunate than the living, who are still alive; but better than both is the one who has not yet been, and has not seen the evil deeds that are done under the sun" (4:1-3).

We have to decide how we will cope with suffering. Shall we opt out of life? To whom can we turn for help? Will our troubles destroy us, or can we survive them and gain a deeper faith in God and a greater love for others?

*What are your most distressing troubles?*

## FAITHFUL LIVING

Psalm 34:1-3 begins with praise of God. Verse 4 testifies to the psalmist's personal experience of God's help in times of trouble. Verses 5-10 combine further testimony with admonition to others to turn to God for help. Verses 11-17, which we will not consider in this lesson, are wisdom teachings about God's dealings with the righteous and the wicked. In verses 18-22, the psalmist returns to personal experience of God's response to suffering and a statement of faith on God's care and salvation. Thus Psalm 34 combines thanksgiving, teaching, witness to God's saving help, and assurance of God's grace.

Psalm 34 is written as an acrostic. The first word of each

line begins with a letter of the Hebrew alphabet, with the letters appearing in alphabetical order. A probable reason for writing a psalm in this way was to make it easy to memorize.

## Seek God's Help

The psalmist testifies,

> I sought the LORD, and he answered me,
> and delivered me from all my fears. . . .
> This poor soul cried, and was heard by the LORD,
> and was saved from every trouble.
> (Psalm 34:4-6)

The Psalms are filled with pleas to God for help. Many petitioners speak of themselves as poor, needy, oppressed, humble, and without human help. In Israel the poor had a special claim on God's mercy and justice:

> I know that the LORD maintains
> the cause of the needy,
> and executes justice for the poor.
> (Psalm 140:12)

Those who had been denied justice elsewhere made pilgrimage to Jerusalem, and in the Temple they sought God's help. In Psalm 34:4, the phrase "sought the LORD" translates a term used for seeking an answer from God through a priest. "*Inquiring* of the Lord" is the way it is sometimes translated. In this case God's answer banished all fears and troubles, and the psalmist praises God.

In Bible times, those without human wealth, power, or protection knew their only help was from God. The Christians I know today who are most likely to seek God's help daily and hourly are those whose incomes cover necessities, not emergencies, and who live where violence and theft are a part of everyday life. They do not have money in the bank or family with the means to help them in times of need. These are also the people most likely to praise God daily for God's goodness and care.

Christians accustomed to being self-sufficient may feel they should not "bother" God with anything less than a major crisis. For years I did not ask God to help me replace resentment of a colleague with love. I saw him so infrequently that my feelings did not seem to matter. Yet what a relief it was when God gave me the grace to meet this person with pleasure.

A pastor friend with a busy schedule asks God's help in overcoming anger and irritation at other drivers who seem bent on keeping him from being on time for meetings. To live as people of God, we need God's help daily to deliver us from our sins and to give us courage to meet life's troubles—both small and great. Small troubles and irritations can eat away at our love and affection for one another and at our joy in living.

We need God's help both for ourselves and for those we love. *Love Letters From Cell 92* (Abingdon, 1995) consists of correspondence between Dietrich Bonhoeffer and his fiancée, Maria von Wedemeyer. Bonhoeffer was a German pastor who resisted Hitler from the beginning and was hanged in April of 1945 after spending two years in prison. In a letter written in August, 1944, Dietrich says to Maria that people who are separated must learn to commend each other to God every day and to put their trust in God.

The psalmist invites us to such an intimate trust in God:

> O taste and see that the LORD is good;
>> happy are those who take refuge in him.
>>>> (Psalm 34:8)

God stands ready to help us in times of trouble. God can help us most effectively when we seek God as the psalmist did in the Temple—where God's people gather. The church at its best is a place where people can share their deepest troubles and celebrate together their greatest joys, rejoicing in God's goodness.

*When and how do you seek God's help? When and how do you rejoice in God's goodness?*

### Fear the Lord

The message of Psalm 34 is not one of universal benevolence. Verse 21 states,

> Evil brings death to the wicked,
>     and those who hate the righteous will be
>         condemned.

God opposes those who practice injustice, cruelty, and oppression.

In the Old Testament, righteousness and wickedness are not seen so much as intrinsic qualities of a person but as a person's actions in relationship to others. The righteous resist the temptation to do wrong. They promote the peace of the community and the well-being of its members, thus preserving faithfully the community's covenant with God.

The wicked plot against the righteous. They act with violence. They oppress the powerless. They do not fear God. But in the view of Scripture, every evil deed will eventually be visited on the one who committed it. As Psalm 7:16 says,

> Their mischief returns upon their own heads,
>     and on their own heads their violence descends.

The righteous live in a community created by the steadfast love of God. One scholar writes, "We do not have terms in English that could reproduce the loyal, intimate, and trusting relationship of life and service, the commitment and devotion of those who are faithful to God. The most frequent expression in the Psalms for this relationship is 'those who fear [God].' "[1]

"The fear of God" is an expression that needs interpretation for us. For those who fear God, God is a living reality. The love of God is central, but awe and fear are not absent; God alone is judge and sovereign. The psalmist can say with confidence,

> O fear the LORD, you his holy ones,
>> for those who fear him have no want.
>>> (Psalm 34:9)

We live in a time when people angrily assert their right to speak hatefully of others, to publish works that would debase the dignity and worth of human beings, to amass arms, to own all they can accumulate with no thought of the needs of others, and to use and despoil the earth without regard for other creatures or for future generations. Do we not need the kind of fear of God that asserts that the living God created people to live together in justice and love and to care for God's creation as good stewards?

*What evidence do you see that God supports the cause of righteousness and justice?*

**God Will Save**

Amid its sweeping assurances of God's help, Psalm 34 presents a realistic picture of life:

> Many are the afflictions of the righteous,
>> but the LORD rescues them from them all.
>>> (Psalm 34:19)

God's rescue is in the midst of afflictions; it is not freedom from afflictions.

In December 1944, Dietrich Bonhoeffer wrote to his fiancée from prison that he was reminded of a children's song about angels keeping watch because he was surrounded by kindly, unseen powers. "I live in a great, unseen realm of whose real existence I'm in no doubt."[2]

> The angel of the LORD encamps
> around those who fear him, and delivers them.
>
> (Psalm 34:7)

The deliverance may not be from physical bonds or dangers; it may be from loneliness, loss of faith, and despair.

From prison it was reported that Bonhoeffer was cheerful and reassuring to the fearful and that he helped strengthen the faith of everyone he encountered. His last words from prison, sent by a prisoner who survived, were, "This is the end—for me, the beginning of life."[3] It could truly be said of him that

> the LORD redeems the life of his servants;
> none of those who take refuge in him
> will be condemned.
>
> (Psalm 34:22)

Verse 20 of Psalm 34 reads,

> He keeps all their bones;
> not one of them will be broken.

This verse is quoted in the account of Jesus' crucifixion in John's Gospel. Jesus' legs were not broken as were the legs of those crucified with him.

The verse suggests the loving care expressed in Jesus'

words, "Are not five sparrows sold for two pennies? Yet not one of them is forgotten in God's sight. . . . Do not be afraid; you are of more value than many sparrows" (Luke 12:6-7).

One who had kinship with the writer of Psalm 34 in bringing the message of God's deliverance was the hymn writer Charles Albert Tindley. He was born a slave in 1856 but served for more than thirty years as the pastor of the church in Philadelphia now named Tindley Temple United Methodist Church.

Most of Tindley's hymns were written between 1901 and 1907. They draw on Scripture and on the experiences of slavery and the hard years following the Civil War. One well-known Tindley hymn has the stanza,

> We are often destitute
>     of the things that life demands,
> want of food and want of shelter,
>     thirsty hills and barren lands;
> we are trusting in the Lord,
>     and according to God's word,
> we will understand it better by
>     and by.[4]

Some experiences of callous brutality, however, we may never understand. The bombing of the Oklahoma City federal building was such an event. At the memorial services for those killed in the bombing, the Core Verse for this lesson was quoted:

> The LORD is near to the brokenhearted,
>     and saves the crushed in spirit.
>                                    (Psalm 34:18)

God offers the brokenhearted and the crushed in spirit salvation through grace by faith. God calls on the church, the community of those who love and fear God, to surround the brokenhearted with love and encouragement, tokens of salvation.

---

**CLOSING PRAYER**
**O God, you are our help in times of trouble. May we reflect your love and care in our presence with others in their times of need. We pray in the name of Jesus. Amen.**

---

[1] From *Theology of the Psalms*, by Hans-Joachim Kraus (Fortress Press, 1992); page 157.

[2] From *Love Letters From Cell 92*, by Dietrich Bonhoeffer (Abingdon Press, 1995); page 269.

[3] From *Love Letters From Cell 92*; page 274.

[4] From "We'll Understand It Better By and By," in *The United Methodist Hymnal* (Copyright © 1989 The United Methodist Publishing House); 525.

### Chapter Four

# NEVER ALONE

**PURPOSE**

To remind us that God knows and cares for us personally

**BIBLE PASSAGE**

Psalm 139:1-14, 23-24

1 O LORD, you have searched me
   and known me.
2 You know when I sit down and when I rise up;
   you discern my thoughts from far away.
3 You search out my path and my lying down,
   and are acquainted with all my ways.
4 Even before a word is on my tongue,
   O LORD, you know it completely.
5 You hem me in, behind and before,
   and lay your hand upon me.
6 Such knowledge is too wonderful for me;
   it is so high that I cannot attain it.

7 Where can I go from your spirit?
   Or where can I flee from your presence?
8 If I ascend to heaven, you are there;
   if I make my bed in Sheol, you are there.

9 **If I take the wings of the morning**
    **and settle at the farthest limits of the sea,**
10 **even there your hand shall lead me,**
    **and your right hand shall hold me fast.**
11 **If I say, "Surely the darkness shall cover me,**
    **and the light around me become night,"**
12 **even the darkness is not dark to you;**
    **the night is as bright as the day,**
    **for darkness is as light to you.**

13 **For it was you who formed my inward parts;**
    **you knit me together in my mother's womb.**
14 **I praise you, for I am fearfully and**
      **wonderfully made.**
  **Wonderful are your works;**
    **that I know very well. . . .**

23 **Search me, O God, and know my heart;**
    **test me and know my thoughts.**
24 **See if there is any wicked way in me,**
    **and lead me in the way everlasting.**

---

### CORE VERSE
*Search me, O God, and know my heart;*
*test me and know my thoughts.*
                   **(Psalm 139:23)**

---

### OUR NEED

    Resident. Client. Employee. Customer. Baby Boomer. Retiree. Divorcee. Patient. Bereaved.

    People today are addressed in many impersonal ways and classified in categories that have little significance for them as individuals. Those doing the classifying usually have a product or service to sell or a responsibility to discharge. Their purpose is not to dehumanize but to get their job done.

Nevertheless, in our increasingly crowded world, individuals can easily feel that they are just labels or numbers. The problem is heightened for those who no longer have close ties with family and friends, who feel expendable at work and without importance in the community. They may believe that their life has little meaning and that their actions do not matter.

"Nobody knows or cares what I do" is an attitude that can lead us to decide we are accountable to no one but ourselves. Then we do not have to vote or to assume responsibilities in community and church or to give what we can to help others. All that is left for us is to try to please ourselves.

Pleasing ourselves, however, may not be easy. Without close relationships and accountability to others, life is often lonely and lacking in a sense of achievement. All of us need to be known personally and to be valued as individuals in order to feel that our lives have real meaning.

*What persons have you known who were led to doubt their own value and worth?*


## FAITHFUL LIVING

Psalm 139 cries out to be read aloud and to be memorized, at least in part. The writer of this psalm could think deeply and feel intensely, and he could create beautiful poetry addressed to God. The psalm is a personal hymn of prayer, praise, and petition.

Verses 1-6 speak of God's knowledge of the psalmist; verses 7-12, of God's presence everywhere. Verses 13-18 reflect that God knows the psalmist because God has created human beings and has provided for their time on earth. (Note: We do not deal with verses 15-18.) Verses 19-22, which are not included in this lesson, are a plea that God will destroy the wicked who oppose God. Verses 23-24 are a petition for God's judgment and God's guidance.

Note that the psalmist addresses God directly and writes out of his personal relationship with God. Nowhere in the psalm does he write about the nature of God or about God's relationship with human beings in an impersonal or abstract way.

Some theologians maintain that the only authentic knowledge of God is personal knowledge. God is so far beyond our understanding that we cannot presume to speak with authority *about* God. But we can speak *to* God, and we can listen to what God has to say to us. We can speak with confidence of our own experiences of God's judgment and grace.

## God Knows Us

> O LORD, you have searched me and known me.
> You know when I sit down and when I rise up;
> you discern my thoughts from far away.
> (Psalm 139:1-2)

Wonder and awe is the psalmist's response to his reflection about God's knowledge of his thoughts, words, and actions. The realization that God knows everything we think, everything we say, everything we do, and everything we are getting ready to say and do is staggering. God also knows our motivations and the reasons for our feelings, thoughts, and actions. We cannot hold that realization in our minds all the time, however. As the psalmist wrote,

> Such knowledge is too wonderful for me;
> it is so high that I cannot attain it.
> (Psalm 139:6)

Even though we believe that God knows us completely, we may hide implications of that belief from ourselves. We may be unwilling to pray about our sins, failures, and depression or about our doubts of God's goodness and God's power to help us. We may not believe God always knows us and is always with us in our unspoken thoughts and feelings. Furthermore, the idea of God's total knowledge of us may make us uncomfortable, as it did the psalmist:

> You hem me in, behind and before,
> and lay your hand upon me.
>                    (Psalm 139:5)

When we bring things before God, we must live with a more realistic, and perhaps more sobering, self-understanding. We may also be led to make difficult and uncomfortable changes in our lives. What we may least expect is that being aware of God's knowledge of us can also lead us to a new appreciation of our gifts, of the possibilities before us, and of our worth as children of God.

I was in theological school with a Chinese woman who, as an infant, had been rescued by Christians from the village garbage dump. She was an unwanted female child left there to die (a custom that still exists in some parts of the world). She lost a hand and several fingers to frostbite, but she learned that in God's sight she was not refuse; she was a person of infinite value.

This woman also had certain expectations placed upon her. The Christian community felt her life had been saved for a purpose—hence her pursuit of a theological education.

We long to be known and understood, and we want our lives to have meaning. Once when I apologized to a friend for talking on at length about what had happened since we had last met, he said, "We all need witnesses to our lives." We need human witnesses, it is true. But we can be assured that we always have a Divine Witness. As the words of the spiritual affirm,

> Nobody knows the trouble I see,
>   Nobody knows but Jesus;
>  oh, nobody knows the trouble I see,
>   glory hallelujah![1]

God knows each of us by name, knows everything that has happened to us, and understands us better than we know and understand ourselves.

*How has your realization that God understands you helped you know and appreciate yourself?*

## God Is With Us

> Where can I go from your spirit?
> Or where can I flee from your presence?
> If I ascend to heaven, you are there;
> if I make my bed in Sheol, you are there.
> (Psalm 139:7-8)

Psalm 139:7-12 affirms the wonder and power of God's presence throughout the universe and acknowledges that no one can escape from God. Amos 9:1-4 also speaks of God's presence everywhere in terms of the impossibility of escaping God's judgment.

Children who have been taught more forcefully of God's judgment than of God's love often interpret God' presence to mean "God sees everything I do wrong." Although the psalmist knows he is accountable before God, his experience is one of trust. He says of the places where he might flee from God,

> Even there your hand shall lead me,
> and your right hand shall hold me fast.
> (Psalm 139:10)

The psalmist has moved far beyond the early idea that God is God of one place and one people and that other places and peoples have other gods. The psalmist also denies the idea that heaven and the underworld are the dwelling places of different deities. He is certain that the one God is Lord of the entire universe.

Those who have returned from hells on earth—hells of addiction and other destructive ways of living—have often testified that God came to them where they were and led them to health and wholeness. Those who meet with great success need equally to realize that God is present with them and that God searches them and knows their heart.

The German theologian Karl Barth wrote, "Every goal that can be reached lies within the realm of the one God and therefore within the realm of His knowledge. . . . We may fall into sin and hell, but whether for salvation or perdition we cannot fall out of the realm of God's knowledge and so out of the realm of His grace and judgment."[2]

For the psalmist, the experience of God's presence was one of trust. I first learned that trust from my mother. After my granddad's death when I was four, my father's travels left my mother and me to spend many nights alone. There was little danger, but Mother had no experience of women and children spending the night without a man in the house. She was anxious; but she said, "Our heavenly Father will be with us. We will trust him."

When the communist regime in China allowed little communication with the West, a former missionary worried about the Christians left behind when he was expelled from the country. Finally, he received a letter. Composed to pass the censor, it said little. But a last word had been added like a signature. That one word, *Emmanuel*, meaning "God is with us," filled this man with joy and hope for his Christian friends in China. The truth behind that one word is all we need to face with courage the dark places of our own lives.

### God Will Lead Us

The psalmist concludes that God knows him completely because God has made him:

> For it was you who formed my inward parts;
> you knit me together in my mother's womb.
>
> (Psalm 139:13)

His response is to praise God and to acknowledge humbly the wonder of his own being:

> I praise you, for I am fearfully and wonderfully made.
>     Wonderful are your works;
> that I know very well.
>
> (Psalm 139:14)

The children in the summer program at our church delight in a song our former pastor Bill Barnes wrote. The chorus goes like this:

> I am a COG.
> A what?
> A child of God!
> You're a COG.
> A what?
> A child of God!
> Let's live that truth.
> Praise God!
> Let's live that truth.

Many of these children receive little affirmation at school or in the community. They soon may discover that the world at large has low expectations of them because of where they live and the color of their skin. They need to know that at God's hand they have been wonderfully made.

The writer of Psalm 139 concludes his psalm by returning to the theme with which he began. Turning from his reverent amazement at God's knowledge of him, God's presence with him, and God's creation of him, he prays,

Search me, O God, and know my heart;
test me and know my thoughts.
See if there is any wicked way in me,
and lead me in the way everlasting.
(Psalm 139:23-24)

The psalmist is asking God to do in the future what God
has already done in the past: to search him and know him,
to test him and help him amend his sinful ways, and to lead
him in the way everlasting. The only appropriate response
to God's unfailing care is to trust God's grace and to follow
God's guidance.
*Where do you believe God is leading you at this particular time
in your life?*

---

**CLOSING PRAYER**
O God, help us to live as those who abide in your presence and as those who treasure the gift of life you have
created in us and in all persons. Lead us, we pray, in the
way everlasting. In Jesus' name. Amen.

---

[1] From "Nobody Knows the Trouble I See," in *The United Methodist Hymnal* (Copyright © 1989 The United Methodist Publishing House); 520.
[2] From *Church Dogmatics*, by Karl Barth (T. and T. Clark, 1936, 1969); Vol.
II, Part 1, page 554.
[3] From "He Leadeth Me: O Blessed Thought," in *The United Methodist
Hymnal* (Copyright © 1989 The United Methodist Publishing House);
128.

### Chapter Five

# TRUST IN GOD

### PURPOSE

To inspire us to tell others of the joy that comes with trusting God

### BIBLE PASSAGE

**Psalm 40:1-5, 9-11, 16-17**

1 I waited patiently for the LORD;
  he inclined to me and heard my cry.
2 He drew me up from the desolate pit,
    out of the miry bog,
  and set my feet upon a rock,
    making my steps secure.
3 He put a new song in my mouth,
    a song of praise to our God.
  Many will see and fear,
    and put their trust in the LORD.
4 Happy are those who make
    the LORD their trust,
  who do not turn to the proud,
    to those who go astray after false gods.
5 You have multiplied, O LORD my God,
    your wondrous deeds and your
      thoughts toward us;
    none can compare with you.

Were I to proclaim and tell of them,
they would be more than can be counted. . . .

9 I have told the glad news of deliverance
in the great congregation;
see, I have not restrained my lips,
as you know, O LORD.
10 I have not hidden your saving help
within my heart,
I have spoken of your faithfulness
and your salvation;
I have not concealed your steadfast love
and your faithfulness
from the great congregation.

11 Do not, O LORD, withhold
your mercy from me;
let your steadfast love and your faithfulness
keep me safe forever. . . .

16 But may all who seek you
rejoice and be glad in you;
may those who love your salvation
say continually, "Great is the LORD!"
17 As for me, I am poor and needy,
but the LORD takes thought for me.
You are my help and my deliverer;
do not delay, O my God.

---

**CORE VERSE**
*Happy are those who make
the LORD their trust.*
*(Psalm 40:4)*

---

## OUR NEED

Listening to radio, watching television, and reading newspapers and magazines can give us the impression that we cannot trust anyone or anything. Besides the alarming news, advertisements insist that we must have security systems for our homes and cars, defensive devices and weapons, and books of advice about how to outwit the forces that are out to get us.

We do need to be prudent in a dangerous world. However, popular opinion can distort the truth in at least two ways. First, it suggests that if we do the right things and buy the right equipment, we will be able to protect ourselves and our families from illness, danger, and disaster. But trust in human aid alone will leave us desolate when death and disaster inevitably come.

A second distortion is that all news is bad—now and forever. In his autobiographical book *Clear Pictures*, Reynolds Price says that when he was growing up, nobody told him that trouble and sorrows do not last forever. He had to learn that truth for himself, slowly and painfully.

Many Christians know that

> weeping may linger for the night,
> but joy comes with the morning.
> (Psalm 30:5c)

We have received good news of great joy. But have we, like the psalmist, shared the good news of God's steadfast love and faithfulness?

*In your community, where do people tell about their experiences of God's goodness?*

## FAITHFUL LIVING

In Psalm 40:1-3, the writer tells how God saved him from desperate trouble and gave him a song of joy. Verses 4-5 speak further of God's blessings on those who put their trust in God.

Verses 6-8, which are not a part of this lesson, may give insight into how this psalm was first presented. Some scholars believe the words in verse 7b, "in the scroll of the book it is written of me," speak of a custom of placing an account of God's deliverance and a psalm one had written in a book in the Temple as a thank offering.

Like the prophets, this psalmist believed that God does not want our burnt offerings but our lives dedicated to God:

> I delight to do your will, O my God;
> your law is within my heart.
> (Psalm 40:8)

Verses 9-10 recount another part of the thank offering: telling the glad news of deliverance to the large congregation gathered in Jerusalem for one of Israel's great festivals.

Psalm 40:11-17 is a prayer the psalmist makes for himself and for all those who seek God. Verses 13-17 are also found as a separate psalm, Psalm 70.

### Wait for the Lord

> I waited patiently for the LORD;
> he inclined to me and heard my cry.
> (Psalm 40:1)

The Scriptures, and especially the Psalms, are full of references to persons who "wait for the Lord." Waiting for the Lord is not just passive sitting around hoping things will get better eventually. Those who wait call on God for help. They are filled with expectation. They trust in God's steadfast love, and they encourage one another:

> Be strong, and let your heart take courage,
>   all you who wait for the LORD.
>                                        (Psalm 31:24)

When Jacob came to the end of his life, he declared, "I wait for your salvation, O LORD" (Genesis 49:18). In despair over the sin and ruin of his people, the prophet Micah declared,

> I will wait for the God of my salvation;
>   my God will hear me.
>                                        (Micah 7:7)

At the time of Jesus' birth, Simeon had been waiting for the Messiah, "looking forward to the consolation of Israel" (Luke 2:25). When he saw the baby Jesus, he praised God and said, "Master, now you are dismissing your servant in peace" (Luke 2:29).

The most dreadful of all possible places to wait for the Lord is the pit. Joseph's brothers threw him into a pit in Dothan before they decided to sell him into slavery. Jeremiah's enemies lowered him into a cistern where he sank in the mud. But the pit of the Psalms, of Ezekiel, and of other parts of Scripture is far more terrible than any of these pits.

The pit is symbolic of shame, death, and the underworld:

> O LORD, you brought up my soul from Sheol,
>   restored me to life from among those gone down
>   to the Pit.
>                                        (Psalm 30:3)

In Psalm 40:2, the writer declares,

> He drew me up from the desolate pit,
>   out of the miry bog,
> and set my feet upon a rock,
>   making my steps secure.

We have images of the pit and the depths of darkness in our own thoughts and feelings. Recently, a friend confided that after she had finished writing a book about her brother's death from AIDS, she had the first depression of her life. She said, "I was in a pit. It wasn't a tunnel; it was a pit, totally dark with no way out."

By God's grace, even in the pit we can know God's presence and grow in trusting God. From out of the depths, the writer of Psalm 130 turned his cry to God and his patient waiting for God into one of the most beautiful poems in Scripture:

> Out of the depths I cry to you, O LORD.
>     Lord, hear my voice! . . .
>
> I wait for the LORD, my soul waits,
>     and in his word I hope;
> my soul waits for the Lord
>     more than those who watch for the morning,
>     more than those who watch for the morning.
>                                    (Psalm 130:1-2, 5-6)

The writer of Psalm 40 had his hope fulfilled. God brought him out of the pit and placed his feet upon a rock, a secure footing for his journey. Jesus' parable of the houses built on rock and sand points out that when a house is built upon the rock, it can withstand the storms that beat upon it. As Psalm 18:2 declares, "The LORD is my rock, my fortress, and my deliverer."

*What experiences have you had of being in the pit? of waiting for God? of having your feet placed upon the rock?*

**Tell the Congregation**

God not only lifted the psalmist out of the pit and set his feet upon a rock; God gave him a new song to sing:

> He put a new song in my mouth,
>     a song of praise to our God.
> Many will see and fear,
>     and put their trust in the LORD.
>
> Happy are those who make
>     the LORD their trust.
> (Psalm 40:3-4)

God's wondrous deeds, the psalmist sings, are "more than can be counted" (40:5).

The psalmist reports to God that in the great congregation assembled in Jerusalem, he has witnessed faithfully to God's steadfast love for him:

> I have told the glad news of deliverance
>     in the great congregation. . . .
> I have spoken of your faithfulness and your
>         salvation;
> I have not concealed your steadfast love and your
>     faithfulness.
> (Psalm 40:9-10)

Telling others about what God had done for him was part of the psalmist's thank offering to God. Israel's worship celebrated God's wonderful deeds in the history of God's people, but God's mercy to individuals was also a part of worship and praise. By offering his testimony in the congregation and adding his written psalm to the Temple record, the psalmist became a part of the great cloud of witnesses who forever encourage the faith and trust of others.

When we tell about God's grace to us, we make visible for

others God's love and God's power to turn hopelessness into trust and joy. The desolate pits we fall into today are different in detail from those the palmists experienced. We need to hear stories of God's deliverance from the particular pits that bedevil us. We need to rejoice in the blessings in our lives today, such as a child who has finally made a B, a cancer patient whose illness is in remission, or adult siblings who have reunited after a long estrangement.

I have been a part of congregations where the pastor and two or three other saints of the church were the only people who talked about what God is doing. The gospel message is crippled in such a setting. One gets the impression that God belongs to the past and is off duty most of the time in the present.

The God revealed in Scripture acts with steadfast love and faithfulness to liberate, to save, to correct, to help, and to heal—in the past, in the present, and in every conceivable future. Jesus said, "My Father is still working, and I also am working" (John 5:17). In telling about what God has done for us, we make clear to ourselves and to others that we serve a living God.

The purpose for gathering as congregations of God's people is to celebrate what God has done and what God is now doing, to praise and worship God, and to carry on God's work in the world. The way we organize and program ourselves must not become a barrier to witnessing to God's grace.

My Sunday school class is a place where members share their lives with one another. In other small groups in the church and in congregational worship, we weep together, laugh together, praise God together, and are strengthened in our trust in God.

To share our lives in this way, we must believe that Jesus came to bring God's love to all people and that God loves and accepts each one of us. Trust in God's love creates trust in one another. As we tell our stories, our knowledge of

God's wondrous deeds is multiplied. We learn that God has the power to deliver us from—or to be with us in the midst of—illness, bereavement, poverty, divorce, imprisonment, abuse, rape, addiction, loss of employment, and even success. When we tell our stories to one another, we become one of the messengers of whom the prophet wrote,

> How beautiful upon the mountains
> are the feet of the messenger
> who announces peace,
> who brings good news,
> who announces salvation,
> who says to Zion, "Your God reigns."
> (Isaiah 52:7)

*What stories of God's steadfast love and faithfulness do you have to tell?*

### Trust God's Faithfulness

We like to think that every problem has a solution and that once solved, a problem will stay solved. The Scriptures give a more realistic picture of life. Even when celebrating God's grace and God's deliverance, the psalmist must continue to pray for salvation from sin and suffering. Thus he relies on God's steadfast love and faithfulness even when encompassed by evil and overtaken by iniquity (Psalm 40:11-12).

Like those in Alcoholics Anonymous who recognize that they will always be recovering alcoholics, we need to recognize that we will always be recovering sinners. Furthermore, we, and all those we love, will die someday. Suffering is a part of earthly life.

The psalmist continues to pray for deliverance, but his prayer is grounded in the hope and trust that come from what he has already experienced of God's grace. The psalmist knew, as Paul would say later, that we have the treasure of God's light in clay jars. We live in the tension of already possessing and yet still waiting for what God will do.

Yet, with the psalmist and with Paul, we can say, "Thanks be to God" for the divine faithfulness in life. With God as our deliverer, we can live to the fullest. If the pit should be our lot, the testimony of others to God's grace can give us hope and patience. In the congregation of God's people, we can declare with joy God's steadfast love to us. Confidently waiting for what God will yet reveal, we pray with the psalmist,

> May all who seek you
>     rejoice and be glad in you;
> may those who love your salvation
>     say continually, "Great is the LORD!"
>                         (Psalm 40:16)

---

**CLOSING PRAYER**

**O God, help me tell about your faithfulness with such thankfulness and joy that others may discover the security, the hope, and the happiness that come from trusting you. In Jesus' name. Amen.**

---

### Chapter Six

# VALUING GOD'S WORD

### PURPOSE

To help us acknowledge that obedience to God's Word is the way to liberty and happiness

### BIBLE PASSAGE
**Psalm 119:1-16, 45, 105, 129-130**

1 Happy are those whose way is blameless,
    who walk in the law of the LORD.
2 Happy are those who keep his decrees,
    who seek him with their whole heart,
3 who also do no wrong,
    but walk in his ways.
4 You have commanded your precepts
    to be kept diligently.
5 O that my ways may be steadfast
    in keeping your statutes!
6 Then I shall not be put to shame,
    having my eyes fixed on
        all your commandments.
7 I will praise you with an upright heart,
    when I learn your righteous ordinances.
8 I will observe your statutes;
    do not utterly forsake me.

9 How can young people keep their way pure?
By guarding it according to your word.
10 With my whole heart I seek you;
do not let me stray from your
commandments.
11 I treasure your word in my heart,
so that I may not sin against you.
12 Blessed are you, O LORD;
teach me your statutes.
13 With my lips I declare
all the ordinances of your mouth.
14 I delight in the way of your decrees
as much as in all riches.
15 I will meditate on your precepts,
and fix my eyes on your ways.
16 I will delight in your statutes;
I will not forget your word. . . .

45 I shall walk at liberty,
for I have sought your precepts. . . .

105 Your word is a lamp to my feet
and a light to my path. . . .

129 Your decrees are wonderful;
therefore my soul keeps them.
130 The unfolding of your words gives light;
it imparts understanding to the simple.

---

**CORE VERSE**
*Your word is a lamp to my feet
and a light to my path.*
*(Psalm 119:105)*

---

*· Jesus — Love the lord with all your heart*

*— Love thy neebor as thyself*

## OUR NEED

Every waking moment we are choosing what we will think, what we will feel, and what we will do. Many of our choices are not conscious ones. Yet they are shaped by values that we have made a part of our lives.

For example, what value do we place on people in general? on particular groups of people? on people we know? Those values determine what we feel, think, and do in our daily encounters with others and in our response to news about people.

Likewise, our values determine how we relate to other creatures of the earth, to the environment, to things, to work, to leisure, to the community, to government, and to ourselves. Do we believe wealth, power over others, and fame are measures of worth? Do we value trustworthiness and integrity? Is kindness and caring an innate part of our being? What value do we place on life itself?

Our answers to these questions reveal our values, and our values help decide our way of life. The question then becomes, Who and what shape our values? Parents and family are key teachers. But as adults do we adopt the values of those around us? of the media? of the company we work for? of groups we belong to?

People today can, in Paul's words, feel "tossed to and fro and blown about by every wind of doctrine" (Ephesians 4:14). We can lack inner principles to guide us in the complexities of today's world. We may wonder if our faith can help us, if the Bible has relevance for life today. Our Bible passage, Psalm 119, urges us to make God's Word the guiding principle of our lives.

*What most strongly influences your thoughts, feelings, actions, and decision making?*

# FAITHFUL LIVING

I first became aware of Psalm 119 at the age when Sunday school teachers and parents encourage children to learn an entire psalm. Psalm 117, with its two verses, was highly favored for this undertaking. Nearby Psalm 117, we children discovered Psalm 119. We noted with awe its 176 verses and wondered if anyone in all the world had ever memorized Psalm 119.

The psalm stands as unique in its form as well as in its length. It is composed of twenty-two eight-line stanzas, one for each of the twenty-two letters of the Hebrew alphabet. Every line of each stanza begins with the letter for that stanza: eight words beginning with *aleph,* eight with *beth,* and so on through the alphabet.

The psalm also uses eight words that mean *torah,* that is, instruction or law. In the New Revised Standard Version of the Bible, these words are translated "commandments," "law," "decrees," "statutes," "ordinance(s)," "precepts," "words," and "promise." The plan of the psalm is to use a different one of these eight words in each of the eight lines of every stanza. That plan is not carried out perfectly, but there are few deviations from it in the whole psalm.

The form of the psalm prevents it from being a poem with unity and progression of development. Scholars speak of Psalm 119 as being like an anthology or a necklace of short Wisdom teachings; hymns; and songs of confession, lament, thanksgiving, and trust. It was a work of devotion used for teaching as well as for celebrating the wonder and value of God's Word. Psalm 119 was probably written after the people of Israel had returned from exile.

In the volume *Psalms* in the Interpretation series of commentaries, James Luther Mays offers this overview of the whole psalm: "*God is the teacher (vv. 33-39).* Creation is the classroom (vv. 89-91, 73). The students are the servants of God (vv. 17, 23, 124f.). The lesson is the 'law' of God (vv. 97-100). Learning is the way of life (vv. 9-16)."[1]

## Learn From God's Word

In the Old Testament the Hebrew word for God's instruction for the people of Israel is usually *torah* or, referring to the first five books of the Bible, *Torah*. *Law* is the English word most often used to translate the Hebrew. Since Psalm 119 is about the Torah, it has traditionally been thought of as a psalm praising God's law.

The meanings and use of words change, however; and our present understanding of the word *law* no longer does justice to the meaning of torah. *Instruction* or *guidance* is a better translation. The Torah includes stories about what God has done and will continue to do for God's people as well as statements about what God requires and how God expects us to live. The Ten Commandments are at the heart of the Torah.

Psalm 119 does not describe what the torah is but speaks of its benefits and tells how the writer and others respond to God's Word. In Psalm 119:1-16, the psalmist mentions treasuring God's Word, taking delight and happiness in it, walking in God's Word, keeping it, observing it, meditating on it, declaring it, learning it, and seeking God.

The torah as it is understood in the Old Testament is not rigid, barren, and legalistic. It tells of God's wondrous works (Psalm 119:27). It is better than gold and silver (verse 72). It gives happiness (verses 1-2), life (verse 40), and salvation (verse 41). God's Word does not enslave, it frees:

> I shall walk at liberty,
> for I have sought your precepts.
> (Psalm 119:45)

Obeying God's Word brings freedom from hate, greed, dishonesty, deliberate unkindness, a need to dominate others, and many other sins that bind and enslave. Jesus said, "If you continue in my word, you are truly my disciples; and you will know the truth, and the truth will make you free" (John 8:31-32).

Accepting the invitation to become a learner means loving God with our minds. Faith seeks understanding. We are willing to study, to meditate on God's Word, and to try to discern God's message for us. We open our minds to new insights.

One always comes to God's Word as a learner, or a disciple; and God is always a part of the teaching:

> Teach me, O LORD, the way of your statutes,
> and I will observe it to the end.
>
> (Psalm 119:33)

Moreover, the teaching and learning of God's Word needs to take place daily among people of all ages. The teaching responsibility is not entrusted to priests, pastors, and professional teachers only. Following the commandment to love God, Deuteronomy 6:7-9 gives instructions about God's words, including: "Recite them to your children and talk about them when you are at home and when you are away, when you lie down and when you rise."

Whether we speak of law, torah, or God's Word, the teaching is always God's. Together we come to God's Word as learners, sharing our wisdom with one another. We come expecting our learning to be a lifelong commitment and joy. But we do not learn from God when we believe we own the truth and that our interpretation of the Word is the only acceptable one.

We are blessed when we say "yes" to Jesus' invitation and learn with others in the mind and spirit of Christ. "Take my yoke upon you, and learn from me; for I am gentle and humble in heart, and you will find rest for your souls" (Matthew 11:29).

*What are the most wonderful and helpful things you have learned from God's Word?*

## Seek With Your Whole Heart

> With my whole heart I seek you;
>   do not let me stray from your commandments.
> I treasure your word in my heart,
>   so that I may not sin against you.
>                                     (Psalm 119:10-11)

In the Scriptures the heart is viewed as the deep center of a human being. The heart is where one knows joy and sorrow, thanksgiving and fear. In the heart are motives, intentions, ambitions, plans, thoughts, decisions, meditation, and reflection. The heart can be the site both of evil and of good. Only God can know the heart completely.

Some Scripture passages from near the time of the Exile speak of God's law being in the human heart, not only on scrolls and tablets of stone. Jeremiah 31:33 says that the time is coming when God will make a new covenant: "I will put my law within them, and I will write it on their hearts; and I will be their God, and they shall be my people."

Psalm 37:30-31 and Psalm 40:8 as well as many verses in Psalm 119 assert that God's Word must be present in the heart. Unless we hold God's teaching and God's will for us at the very center of our being, we will not faithfully trust God and obey God's instruction. Jesus teaches, especially in the Sermon on the Mount, that sin and goodness come, not from outside, but from what is in the heart.

Psalm 119 and other psalms also urge us to seek God with our whole heart. A divided heart is not steadfast. It is like those Jesus describes who try to serve two masters.

Commitment to the Word of God, then, can never be superficial or a grudging compliance with external rules. We are called, in the words of Paul, to "be transformed by the renewing of your minds, so that you may discern what is the will of God—what is good and acceptable and perfect" (Romans 12:2).

Charles Wesley wrote a hymn about such transformation:

> O for a heart to praise my God,
> a heart from sin set free,
> a heart that always feels thy blood
> so freely shed for me.[2]

*What thoughts and intentions of your heart would you pray for God to transform?*

## Walk in God's Way

According to Psalm 119, God's Word is not for standing still. It does not just stay in church on Sunday mornings. It is living and active. It goes with us on our journey through life and sets out for us the path God wants us to take:

> Happy are those whose way is blameless,
> who walk in the law of the LORD.
> (Psalm 119:1)

Throughout Psalm 119, the psalmist, in trust, addresses God directly and personally with the earnest desire to understand the path God has set out and to obey God in following that path:

> Lead me in the path of your commandments,
> for I delight in it.
> (Psalm 119:35)

God's Word gives the light needed to walk in God's way. Light brings understanding:

> The unfolding of your words gives light;
> it imparts understanding to the simple.
> (Psalm 119:130)

Light also gives reassurance and banishes fear:

> Your word is a lamp to my feet
> and a light to my path.
>> (Psalm 119:105)

God's Word can keep one from going astray:

> When I think of your ways,
> I turn my feet to your decrees.
>> (Psalm 119:59)

But God's grace also can restore the straying one:

> I have gone astray like a lost sheep; seek out your
> servant,
> for I do not forget your commandments.
>> (Psalm 119:176)

God's way is also a never failing source of joy, the delight of the heart:

> Your decrees are my heritage forever;
> they are the joy of my heart.
>> (Psalm 119:111)

Such is the testimony of those who have studied God's Word, who have kept it in their hearts, and who have walked in God's ways.

*How does God's Word bring liberty and happiness to your life?*

**CLOSING PRAYER**

Blessed Lord, you have caused all holy Scriptures to be written for our learning. Grant us so to hear, read, mark, and inwardly digest them that we may embrace and ever hold fast the blessed hope of everlasting life, which you have given to us in our Savior Jesus Christ, in whose name we pray. Amen.

[1] From *Psalms*, by James Luther Mays, in Interpretation: A Bible Commentary for Preaching and Teaching (John Knox Press, 1994); page 381.
[2] From "O for a Heart to Praise My God," in *The United Methodist Hymnal* (Copyright © 1989 The United Methodist Publishing House); 417.

### Chapter Seven

# SEEKING FORGIVENESS

### PURPOSE

To call us to repentance for our sins and so to the experience of God's forgiveness

### BIBLE PASSAGE

**Psalm 51:1-13, 17**

1 Have mercy on me, O God,
   according to your steadfast love;
   according to your abundant mercy
   blot out my transgressions.
2 Wash me thoroughly from my iniquity,
   and cleanse me from my sin.
3 For I know my transgressions,
   and my sin is ever before me.
4 Against you, you alone, have I sinned,
   and done what is evil in your sight,
   so that you are justified in your sentence
   and blameless when you pass judgment.
5 Indeed, I was born guilty,
   a sinner when my mother conceived me.

6 You desire truth in the inward being;
   therefore teach me wisdom in my secret heart.

7 Purge me with hyssop, and I shall be clean;
    wash me, and I shall be whiter than snow.
8 Let me hear joy and gladness;
    let the bones that you have crushed rejoice.
9 Hide your face from my sins,
    and blot out all my iniquities.

10 Create in me a clean heart, O God,
    and put a new and right spirit within me.
11 Do not cast me away from your presence,
    and do not take your holy spirit from me.
12 Restore to me the joy of your salvation,
    and sustain in me a willing spirit.

13 Then I will teach transgressors your ways,
    and sinners will return to you. . . .

17 The sacrifice acceptable to God is a broken spirit;
    a broken and contrite heart,
      O God, you will not despise.

---

**CORE VERSE**
*Create in me a clean heart, O God,*
*and put a new and right spirit within me.*
*(Psalm 51:10)*

---

## OUR NEED

Every one of us old enough to be in an adult class is aware of falling short of our expectations of ourselves—and of God's expectations of us. We have hurt those we love. We have told interesting bits of news, then realized we have betrayed a confidence. We have been dishonest with ourselves and with others in small things—or in large things. In many different ways, we have been unfaithful to God and to one another.

What we have left undone may haunt us even more than what we have done. We may feel guilt and regret for failing someone who has died or who is no longer with us. When we hear of a person of our own age and circumstance in life whose hard work and self-giving love have made a real difference in the world, we think, *If I had been more unselfish, I could have done that.* With every passing week, we may regret things we are failing to do.

Do we sin against ourselves, damaging our bodies, minds, and emotions by the way we live—by our poor choices, neglect, or overindulgence? We may know we have squandered, or failed to develop, gifts and opportunities God has given us. We are harried by persistent sins and shortcomings that always seem to be with us.

Unless repentance, forgiveness, and renewal are a part of our lives, our sins can overwhelm us and destroy us. For penitent sinners, Psalm 51 is an example to learn from and a prayer to make our own.

***How have you fallen short of your own expectations?***

## FAITHFUL LIVING

Over the centuries Psalm 51 has been important in Christian worship and devotion. It is traditionally the Ash Wednesday psalm and is also used throughout the year in prayer and confession. Worshipers will know verses from Psalm 51 even when they have made no effort to memorize them.

Psalm 51:1-2 is a prayer for God's mercy and forgiveness. Verses 3-5 acknowledge the psalmist's sin and guilt. Verses 6-9 are a prayer for cleansing and forgiveness; verses 10-12, a prayer for a clean heart, a willing spirit, and the joy of God's salvation. In verse 13, the psalmist promises to teach sinners God's ways. Verses 15-17 speak of the kind of sacrifice that is acceptable to God.

Those who edited the Psalms have titled Psalm 51 as David's confession at the time of the events of 2 Samuel 11 and 12. The worshiping community who used this psalm saw it as describing the way God related to David and thus to all sinners. A review of David's story in 2 Samuel 11–12 shows the devastation of sin, the urgent need for repentance, and the hope of God's grace.

While David's army was away fighting, David saw and desired Bathsheba, the wife of Uriah, a soldier. David took Bathsheba and sired a child. Then, in an effort to cover his sin, David sent for Uriah. But Israel's soldiers vowed celibacy in the conviction that God fought with them. Uriah was devout and refused to break his vow, even with his own wife.

David then sent a message to Uriah's commander, Joab, to place Uriah in the thick of the fighting and to withdraw so that Uriah would be killed. The stratagem succeeded, with Uriah being killed and other valiant men as well. After a period of mourning, Bathsheba and David were married.

The prophet Nathan came to David and told him a story: A poor man had one ewe lamb. The lamb was like a pet in his household, eating and sleeping with his family. One day a visitor came to the house of a neighboring rich man. This man had vast flocks and herds; but he took the poor man's pet lamb, killed it, and served it to his visitor.

"Then David's anger was greatly kindled against the man. He said to Nathan, 'As the LORD lives, the man who has done this deserves to die; he shall restore the lamb fourfold, because he did this thing, and because he had no pity.' Nathan said to David, 'You are the man!' " (2 Samuel 12:5-7).

Then "David said to Nathan, 'I have sinned against the LORD' " (2 Samuel 12:13).

Bathsheba's child became seriously ill. For seven days, David fasted, lay prostrate on the ground, and prayed for the child. But the child died.

David had violated Bathsheba. He had tried to make

Uriah break his vows. He had induced Joab to be his agent in Uriah's murder. In his child's death, David reaped the immediate results of his sin. Possibly, he lost integrity and authority in his own household as well. His sons committed incest and murder and rebelled against him.

Nevertheless, Nathan conveyed God's promise that David himself would not die and that his line would continue. He and Bathsheba had another child, Solomon, whom the Lord loved.

### I Have Sinned

David's actions toward Bathsheba and Uriah would have been standard operating procedure for many kings. But Israel's king was accountable to God. Sin is a violation of God's will; thus the psalmist said,

> Against you, you alone, have I sinned;
> and done what is evil in your sight,
> so that you are justified in your sentence
> and blameless when you pass judgment.
> (Psalm 51:4)

Sins against God's people, against God's creatures, and against God's earth are, first of all, sins against God. They violate the sacred worth conferred on all things when at Creation, God called them good. Moreover, sin violates the righteousness, justice, and peace of the community God intends for human beings.

The psalmist acknowledged and confessed his sin:

> For I know my transgressions,
> and my sin is ever before me.
> (Psalm 51:3)

When confronted with his sin, David took no thought for public opinion or for how he might have avoided getting caught. He did not assert that he was no worse than the average king and better than most. God's judgment enabled him to see the enormity of what he had done when he used his power as king to take what he wanted with no regard for God or for others.

Nathan's story of the poor man with the one ewe lamb enlivened David's imagination and enabled him to see someone else's life with sympathy and concern. Both small, daily hurts and atrocities that shock the world begin with looking on others without empathy or sympathy. Widening the circle of those who care is doing God's work in the world.

The psalmist also said,

> Indeed, I was born guilty,
>     a sinner when my mother conceived me.
> 
> (Psalm 51:5)

Both verses 4 and 5 refer to the pervasiveness of sin and to the condition of sinfulness. Our problem is not just a few offenses for which we need pardon but the condition of our whole being. What has happened to us from birth—things for which we are not to blame—has helped shape us. Abused children, for instance, often grow up to be abusers. They need to be delivered from their condition as well as from their acts.

We are also conditioned by society around us. One of my persistent sins is to go on living in comfort when so many of God's children are in great need. Without God's judgment and grace, we are blind to our own condition. As John Newton wrote,

> 'Twas grace that taught my heart to fear,
>     and grace my fears relieved.[1]

Jesus' life reveals what God calls us to be and to do. Jesus' death reveals the dreadful cost of turning away from love. His resurrection reveals God's power and grace to overcome sin.

*How has God helped you to acknowledge sin in your life?*

**Forgive Me, O God**

> Have mercy on me, O God,
>     according to your steadfast love;
> according to your abundant mercy
>     blot out my transgressions.
>
> (Psalm 51:1)

God's steadfast love and mercy make possible the psalmist's confession of sin. Without God's grace and the possibility of forgiveness, we would not be led to repentance. I know of parents who have disowned a child, but I have never heard of such actions bringing a change of heart or reconciliation. In contrast, God's reconciling love in Christ brings repentance.

We have Jesus' assurance that when we repent and confess our sins, we will receive God's grace. The man who cried, "God, be merciful to me, a sinner!" went down to his home justified rather than the man who boasted in his own self-righteousness (Luke 18:9-14). In Psalm 51:15-17, the psalmist is saying that God wants a humble offering of ourselves, not pride in our own virtue or in our religious observance:

> The sacrifice acceptable to God is a broken spirit;
>     a broken and contrite heart,
>         O God, you will not despise.
>
> (Psalm 51:17)

Our relationship with God is limited and our relationships with others are limited when we are unwilling to ask, "Am I at fault?" or to acknowledge being in the wrong. Jeremiah wrote about the impending ruin of God's people:

> No one repents of wickedness,
> saying, "What have I done!"
> (Jeremiah 8:6)

When we repent and confess our sins, we are making a statement of faith. We affirm the justice and excellence of God's requirements of us and acknowledge God's right to our obedience. We also ask God to do what we cannot do for ourselves: cleanse us from guilt and sin. Verse 6 of Psalm 51,

> You desire truth in the inward being;
> therefore teach me wisdom in my secret heart

is probably a prayer for God to reform our motives, to free us from self-deception, and to help us grow in self-understanding.

Peter denied Jesus three times. Judas betrayed Jesus. Each regretted his act, and Judas hanged himself. But Peter did not separate himself from the other disciples or from Jesus. In repentance and humility, in the midst of God's people, he allowed God to continue to work in his life.

*What experiences lead you to true repentance and confession?*

### Create in Me a New Spirit

The psalmist prays in the conviction that God offers renewal as well as forgiveness:

> Create in me a clean heart, O God,
> and put a new and right spirit within me.
> (Psalm 51:10)

In the Old Testament the word *create* speaks of what only God can do. God creates, bringing into being what did not exist before. God also creates by transforming what is already present so that it becomes something new. During the Exile, Ezekiel wrote about God's promise to transform Israel: "A new heart I will give you, and a new spirit I will put within you; and I will remove from your body the heart of stone and give you a heart of flesh" (Ezekiel 36:26).

We cannot live as transformed people in a new and right spirit unless we remain in touch with the guiding and sustaining power of God's Holy Spirit. The psalmist prayed,

> Restore to me the joy of your salvation,
> and sustain in me a willing spirit.
> (Psalm 51:12)

The Holy Spirit is present with us as individuals, but the power of the Spirit can move most strongly in congregations of God's people. We can help one another know what God is calling us to be and to do. Together we can confess our sins, strengthen one another's faith, and celebrate the joy of God's salvation.

## CLOSING PRAYER

Most merciful God,
we confess that we have sinned
 against you
in thought, word, and deed,
by what we have done, and
by what we have left undone.
We have not loved you with our
 whole heart,
We have not loved our
 neighbors as ourselves.
We are truly sorry
 and we humbly repent.
For the sake of your Son
 Jesus Christ,
have mercy on us and forgive
 us;
that we may delight in your
 will,
and walk in your ways,
to the glory of your name.
        Amen.[2]

---

[1] From "Amazing Grace," in *The United Methodist Hymnal* (Copyright © 1989 The United Methodist Publishing House); 378.
[2] From *The United Methodist Hymnal* (Copyright © 1989 The United Methodist Publishing House); 890.

**Chapter Eight**

# WORSHIP AND WITNESS

### PURPOSE
To help us celebrate God's power and goodness

### BIBLE PASSAGE
**Psalm 96:1-13**

1 O sing to the LORD a new song;
     sing to the LORD, all the earth.
2 Sing to the LORD, bless his name;
     tell of his salvation from day to day.
3 Declare his glory among the nations,
     his marvelous works among all the peoples.
4 For great is the LORD, and greatly
          to be praised;
     he is to be revered above all gods.
5 For all the gods of the peoples are idols,
     but the LORD made the heavens.
6 Honor and majesty are before him;
     strength and beauty are in his sanctuary.

7 Ascribe to the LORD, O families of the peoples,
     ascribe to the LORD glory and strength.
8 Ascribe to the LORD the glory due his name;
     bring an offering, and come into his courts.

71

9 Worship the LORD in holy splendor;
    tremble before him, all the earth.

10 Say among the nations, "The LORD is king!
    The world is firmly established;
      it shall never be moved.
    He will judge the peoples with equity."
11 Let the heavens be glad, and let the earth rejoice;
    let the sea roar, and all that fills it;
12    let the field exult, and everything in it.
  Then shall all the trees of the forest
      sing for joy
13    before the LORD; for he is coming,
    for he is coming to judge the earth.
  He will judge the world with righteousness,
    and the peoples with his truth.

---

**CORE VERSE**
*Sing to the LORD, bless his name;*
*tell of his salvation from day to day.*
*(Psalm 96:2)*

---

### OUR NEED

Forces of hate in the world are saying, "Only people like us and people who think as we do deserve to live." Modern weapons give those forces power to kill and injure great numbers of people—wherever they choose to strike.

Forces of self-aggrandizement and indifference to the well-being of all people are saying, "Only people like us deserve to live well." Modern media give these forces the power to spread half truths, to instill fear, and to play on self-interest in order to control wealth for the benefit of their kind of people. What they are saying and doing helps fuel the forces of hate.

Popular voices are saying, "You have to go with the opinion polls." "The one with the most toys wins." "Live fast; die young." "Do it now." "Shop till you drop." "You can't fight city hall." For these voices, all there is and all that matters is what comes to the surface of popular culture: "Watch out for your own interests." "Enjoy yourself if you can." "Who cares what happens after you're dead?"

As Christians, we live with these forces and these voices. Some purveyors of indifference and hate even identify themselves as Christian. No wonder a friend said, "I'm so afraid about what's happening in the world."

What can we say and do in a world like ours? How can we demonstrate the power of love? The psalmists proclaimed, "The LORD is king!" In a world of darkness and trouble, they said, "Sing to the LORD a new song."

*Where do you see the need to proclaim the message, "The Lord is king"?*


## FAITHFUL LIVING

Psalm 96 was likely written after the people of Israel returned from exile. Each year, at the beginning of the Feast of Tabernacles or Booths, Psalm 96 was probably sung in a solemn procession to pay homage to God as king.

First Chronicles 16:23-33, also written after the Exile, includes Psalm 96, with minor variations in wording, as a psalm sung by Asaph and his kindred at the celebration of the bringing of the ark of the covenant to Jerusalem in the time of David.

Psalm 96 is a hymn of praise to God as ruler and judge of all the earth. Verses 1-3 are a call to praise God in song. Verses 4-6 give reasons for praising God. Verses 7-9 are another call to glorify God. Verses 10-13 proclaim God as king and tell what God has done and will continue to do as creator and righteous judge of all the earth.

## "O Sing to the LORD"

> O sing to the LORD a new song;
> sing to the LORD, all the earth.
> (Psalm 96:1)

Some scholars think new songs spoken of in Scripture were newly written songs composed as thank offerings to God. In any case, a God who is continually at work for the good of every creature cannot be praised adequately with old songs only. As God's people, we need to sing old songs with new understanding of their meaning. We need to sing new songs that celebrate the new works God is doing among us. We also need to offer our own songs—however expressed—to give thanks for God's goodness to us as individuals.

Psalms that sing a new song usually celebrate God's goodness in the past, glory in God's daily presence, and express confidence that the future will be governed by God's righteousness and grace. Singing to the Lord can lift our hearts so that both our emotions and our intellects are engaged in praising God's power and goodness. Our duty and our joy as congregations of God's people and as individuals is to sing to the Lord.

John Wesley's directions for singing, first given in a 1761 hymnal, include the following directions:

III. See that you join with the congregation as frequently as you can. Let not a slight degree of weakness or weariness hinder you. If it is a cross to you, take it up, and you will find it a blessing.
IV. Sing lustily and with a good courage. Beware of singing as if you were half dead, or half asleep; but lift up your voice with strength. . . .
VII. Above all sing spiritually. Have an eye to God in every word you sing. Aim at pleasing him more than yourself, or any other creature. . . . So shall your singing be such as the

Lord will approve here, and reward you when he cometh in the clouds of heaven.[1]

The psalmist calls the people to

> Sing to the LORD, bless his name;
> tell of his salvation from day to day.
> (Psalm 96:2)

Blessing God's name (verse 2) and giving God the glory due his name (verse 8) grow out of the special relationship the people of Israel had with God because God had entrusted them with his name. When "LORD" is printed in the Bible with a capital letter followed by small capitals, it stands for YHWH. That is the name God gave Moses when he asked at the time of his call on Mount Horeb / Sinai whom he should say sent him to the Israelites in Egypt.

God freely and graciously makes his name known. Through knowing God's name, Israel could relate to a personal God rather than to an impersonal force. God's name denotes the one revealed to Israel through God's presence and through God's faithfulness in keeping promises.

God's name has been given to Israel, but it may not be used for magic or cursing or in any effort to manipulate God or human beings. God's name is holy; and though given, it is still God's. When persons die and nations are destroyed, their names are forgotten. But the name of the Lord endures forever, giving comfort and hope.

Glory and blessing are due God's name because through it Israel has received justice, deliverance, salvation, and wisdom. Israel loves, fears, and trusts God's name; calls on God's name; and shouts for joy at God's name.

Israel blesses God's name by telling of God's salvation from day to day. The Hebrew word used for "telling" in this verse is the verb used for the responsibility of a herald who goes before a commander to give news of victory to waiting people. Every day brings new tidings of God's salvation that call for a new song to celebrate God's wonderful deeds.

*If you wrote a new song to God, what are some of God's deeds you would celebrate?*

### Declare to the Nations

God's salvation is not Israel's secret. The psalmist calls Israel to tell the nations about their God:

> Declare his glory among the nations,
>     his marvelous works among all the peoples.
>                                         (Psalm 96:3)

The most celebrated of God's mighty and glorious acts was delivering the people of Israel from slavery in Egypt and bringing them into the Promised Land. Hearing that story has given hope to oppressed people throughout history, including slaves in the United States.

When Psalm 96 was written, Israel had experienced another great act of God. God had gathered the scattered exiles, brought them back to their own land, and given them the opportunity to rebuild Jerusalem and the Temple. That story gives the assurance that with God's help people can rebuild, even from ruin.

One of our complaints today is that the news media specialize in bad news. The media have no mandate to tell good news; but God's people do: to declare God's glory among the nations, to go into all the world—both near and far—to tell the good news of God's love made known in Jesus Christ.

A reason the psalmist gives for proclaiming God's wonderful works among the nations is that the Lord is great and is to

be revered above all gods.
For all the gods of the peoples are idols,
but the LORD made the heavens.
(Psalm 96:4b-5)

The God of Creation and the God who acts in history cannot be compared to gods that are only idols. In pronouncing God's judgment on Israelites who adopted the worship of idols from their neighbors, Isaiah said in wonder,

They bow down to the work of their hands,
to what their own fingers have made.
(Isaiah 2:8b)

We are not tempted to worship images made of gold, but we are not exempt from worshiping the works of our hands. Our idols may be material things—electronics, automobiles, weapons, houses, clothes. They may be organizations and our place in them—the corporation, the U.S. Congress, the club, even the church.

When we get angry if someone questions the value or usefulness of a human creation, we should beware of idols. When we feel our happiness or our safety depends on a human creation, we should beware of idols. When we refuse to consider change or the possibility of other ways of doing things, we should beware of idols.

Idols prevent us from giving God the glory due his name and from declaring God's glory among all peoples. The families of the earth are called to honor God and to worship God alone.

*In what way can you proclaim God's glory to the people in your world?*

## "The LORD Is King"

> Say among the nations, "The LORD is king!
>     The world is firmly established;
>         it shall never be moved.
>     He will judge the peoples with equity."
>                         (Psalm 96:10)

Psalm 96 proclaims God's reign in the natural world and in the affairs of peoples and nations. To say "The Lord is king" affirms that God's dependability and justice will prevail rather than the capriciousness of other gods or the sinfulness and unreliability of human beings.

Psalmists and prophets hoped for the day when all peoples would acknowledge God's reign and be eager to learn God's ways. Isaiah looked forward to a time when the nations would say,

> Come, let us go up to the mountain of the LORD,
>     to the house of the God of Jacob;
>         that he may teach us his ways
>         and that we may walk in his paths.
>                         (Isaiah 2:3)

In Scripture, the well-being of the natural world is often related to justice, righteousness, and peace in the human world. God's reign brings rejoicing for all creation:

> Let the heavens be glad, and let the earth rejoice;
>     let the sea roar, and all that fills it;
>     let the field exult, and everything in it.
> Then shall all the trees of the forest sing for joy.
>                         (Psalm 96:11-12)

The hymn "Joy to the World" brings the same message:

Joy to the world,
  the Savior reigns!
Let all their songs employ;
  while fields and floods,
rocks, hills, and plains
  repeat the sounding joy.[2]

God's judgment is often thought of as punishment rather than as cause for rejoicing. But in Psalm 96, the whole earth sings before the Lord because

he is coming to judge the earth.
He will judge the world with righteousness,
  and the peoples with his truth.
                              (Psalm 96:13)

People who have suffered the oppressive injustice of earthly power and the burden of their own sinfulness welcome and trust a righteous judge. They look forward to the coming of one who will bring justice and peace.

Churches that use the common lectionary read Psalm 96 at Christmas. On this day, the psalm expresses our joy in Jesus' birth and our hope for the coming of God's kingdom on earth. Charles Wesley's hymn "Rejoice, the Lord Is King" expresses the joyful message of Psalm 96:

Rejoice, the Lord is King!
  Your Lord and King adore;
mortals, give thanks and sing,
  and triumph evermore.

His kingdom cannot fail;
  he rules o'er earth and heaven;
the keys of earth and hell are
  to our Jesus given.[3]

## CLOSING PRAYER

O God, help us rejoice in the wonder and majesty of your creation and give thanks for your righteousness and your goodness to us. With our voices and with our lives help us sing a song that says to all the world, "God reigns." In Jesus' name. Amen.

[1] From "Directions for Singing," in *The United Methodist Hymnal* (Copyright © 1989 The United Methodist Publishing House); vii.

[2] From "Joy to the World," in *The United Methodist Hymnal* (Copyright © 1989 The United Methodist Publishing House); 246.

[3] From "Rejoice, the Lord Is King," in *The United Methodist Hymnal* (Copyright © 1989 The United Methodist Publishing House); 715.